NOBLE PURPOSE

NOBLE PURPOSE

The Joy of Living a Meaningful Life

WILLIAM DAMON

Templeton Foundation Press

Philadelphia & London

Templeton Foundation Press
Five Radnor Corporate Center, Suite 120
100 Matsonford Road
Radnor, Pennsylvania 19087
www.templetonpress.org

Library of Congress Cataloging-in-Publication Data
Damon, William, 1944-
Noble purpose : the joy of living a meaningful life / William Damon.
        p. cm.
Includes bibliographical references.
ISBN 1-932031-54-5 (alk. paper)
1. Conduct of life. 2. Vocation. 3. Life. 4. Meaning (Philosophy).
        I. Title.
        BJ1581.2 .D32 2003
        170—dc21   2003013592

Designed and typeset by Helene Krasney
Printed by McNaughton & Gunn, Inc.
Printed in the United States of America
03 04 05 06 07   10 9 8 7 6 5 4 3 2 1

To Bob and Dottie King and family:

Thriving with purpose!

CONTENTS

INTRODUCTION

To be what is called happy," wrote the nineteenth-century Polish poet Cyprian Norwid, "one should have (a) something to live on, (2) something to live for, (3) something to die for. The lack of one of these results in drama. The lack of two results in tragedy."

This slim volume, authored by renowned Stanford University psychologist William Damon, testifies to the wisdom of those words. In addition to our human needs of sustaining and reproducing our bodies, we humans flourish when also meeting two higher-level needs that today's psychological science is more and more appreciative of: our need to belong, and our need for significance, for meaning, for noble purpose.

Recent American Psychological Association president Martin Seligman observed that a loss of meaning has accentuated the recent epidemic of depression. Finding meaning, he has noted, requires "an attachment to something larger than the lonely self. To the extent that young people now find it hard to take seriously their relationship with God, to care about their relationship with the country, or to be part of a large and abiding family, they will find it very difficult to find meaning in life. To put it another way, the self is a very poor site for finding meaning."

At the peak of her fame and fortune, with 146 tennis championships behind her and married to John Lloyd, Chris Evert reflected, "We get into a rut. We play tennis, we go to a movie, we watch TV, but I keep saying, 'John, there has to be more.'" For the full life, we need more than bread alone.

For psychologist Mihaly Csikszentmihalyi, well-being arises from having one's life focused on an overriding goal, a unifying theme that gives meaning to our lesser goals. For Mother Teresa it was to help the destitute: "Nothing makes you happier than when you really reach out in mercy to someone who is badly hurt," she reflected. Mother Teresa, like so many other purpose-filled people, may not have lived "the good life" in the optimum material sense, but she lived a good, rich life.

Csikszentmihalyi has studied the "flow" experience enjoyed by purposeful artists, physicians, writers, and athletes. When he and his colleagues beeped trial participants at random intervals, their consistent finding was that those who were vegetating, perhaps as couch potatoes in front of the television, reported little of the satisfaction that accompanies the unself-conscious experience of flow. When interrupted while doing something active and purposeful—whether at leisure or work—they more often were totally immersed, unconscious of time, and delightfully engrossed. "In every part and corner of our life, to lose oneself is to be a gainer," noted Robert Louis Stevenson. "To forget oneself is to be happy."

One of the most remarkable people I have known was industrialist John Donnelly, whose company manufactured most car mirrors. Shortly before his death at age seventy-four, he remarked, "What will I have achieved in life if all I have done is to make car mirrors—there has to be more to it than that." So part of his life mission, beyond making safety-enhancing car mirrors, was to create meaningful, involving work experiences. To accomplish this, he pioneered the organization of his employees into self-managed work groups and shared profits with them when times were good. By engaging them in structuring their own work and setting their own goals, he added purpose to their lives, and he made the Donnelly Corporation not only profitable but a place that workers raved about.

But enough from me. William Damon, who has studied what purpose adds to developing lives, is the gentle and wise expert here. He helps us welcome purpose into our everyday lives and into our calling at work. And he helps us appreciate the psychological roots and spiritual fruits of purpose. Let us learn from him, and from the sages whose voices he has assembled.

—DAVID G. MYERS

HOPE COLLEGE

NOBLE PURPOSE

One needs something to believe in,
something for which one can have
whole-hearted enthusiasm.
One needs to feel that one's life has meaning,
that one is needed in this world.

—HANNAH SENESH

PURPOSE IN EVERYDAY LIFE

All of us have moments when we become absorbed in getting something done. It may be something common, such as untying a stubborn knot in your shoelace or cooking a perfect soft-boiled egg. It may be something playful, such as making a tricky golf putt or solving a crossword puzzle. Or it may be something quite serious, such as driving your car home through a sudden ice storm or going to the rescue of a friend who has just been hurt.

Think about how you experience such moments. If you really throw yourself into the endeavor, you will give it your complete attention. You stop thinking about yourself but instead become fascinated by the problem at hand. At the same time, as you

Knowing who we are, why we are here,
and what we're tying to do with our lives
enriches our journey. Whether our purpose
is to serve God, to raise healthy children,
to create a healthier environment, or to play
beautiful music, we are empowered
by the purpose.

—RICHARD J. LEIDER

muster your mental and physical capacities to reach a solution, you may discover powers that you never thought you had—untried talents, new skills, reservoirs of untapped energy. You feel a surge of excitement as you move towards your goal. You lose track of your everyday cares and woes, of where you happen to be, of what time it is, of your own bodily presence—in short, of all the usual shackles of our physical and material world. You may feel that sublime state of spiritual emancipation that some psychologists have termed "flow."[1] While your absorption in the task may feel hard, it also brings you a tangible sense of satisfaction, well-being, and exhilaration.

The examples above—cooking eggs, making golf putts, driving home through storms—are absorbing but transient experiences that people may engage in from time to time. But can you imagine living your whole life with that kind of focus? All of us have that choice. To live in this way means finding large-scale *purposes* that concentrate your talents, skills,

This is the true joy in life,
the being used for a purpose recognized
by yourself as a mighty one;
the being thoroughly worn out before
you are thrown on the scrap heap;
being a Force of Nature
instead of a feverish selfish little clod
of ailments and grievances
complaining that the world will not
devote itself to making you happy.

—George Bernard Shaw

thoughts, and energies in an enduring manner. It means finding something that you truly believe in, something so worth accomplishing that you dedicate yourself to it wholeheartedly, without qualm or self-interest. It means devoting yourself to a cause, or to many causes, that you consider *noble purposes*.

"Noble" does not always mean "heroic," if we take "heroic" to mean pursuing daring, life-endangering adventures, like the mythical knights who fought dragons in days of yore. Noble purpose *can* mean this, and our history books are full of dramatic accounts of courageous acts that saved the day. But noble purpose also may be found in the day-to-day fabric of ordinary existence. A mother caring for her child, a teacher instructing students, a doctor healing patients, a citizen campaigning for a candidate for the sake of improving society—all are pursuing noble purposes. So, too, are the legions of people who dedicate time, care, effort, and worldly goods to charity, to their friends and family, to their communities, and to God.

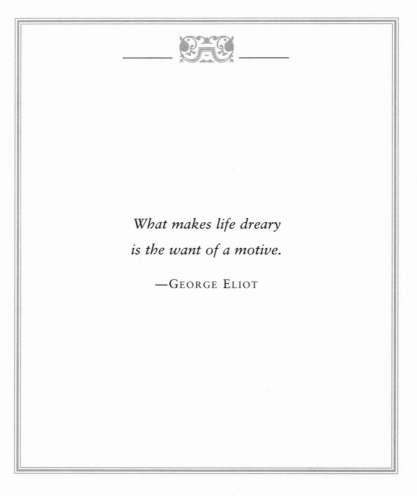

What makes life dreary
is the want of a motive.

—George Eliot

Noble purposes generally are serious affairs—except for a few impassioned golf pros, not many sustain a lifetime of satisfaction and exhilaration by sinking putts—but noble purposes may be found in familiar places and pursued in everyday acts. With the right intention and perspective, a person can transform a mere gesture into a step towards a noble purpose.

Because noble purpose can be such an important dimension in people's lives, scientists have become interested in studying how people acquire and sustain their purposes. Whenever scientists study any phenomenon, they carefully define it, so that there will be no ambiguity in what they are measuring and in what they mean when they put forth conclusions. The following statement captures how scientists define the term "purpose" for the sake of systematic research: "Purpose is a stable and generalized intention to accomplish something both meaningful to the self and of consequence to the world beyond the self."[2]

*Many persons have a wrong idea
of what constitutes true happiness.
It is not attained through self-gratification
but through fidelity to a worthy purpose.*

—HELEN KELLER

This scientific definition draws our attention to the following qualities of purpose:

- Purpose is a goal, but it is more stable and far-reaching than lower-level objectives such as "to get a good dress to wear to the party" or "to find a seat in that crowded restaurant."

- Purpose is a key part of our own personal search for meaning, but it also has an external quality, a desire to make a difference in the world, to contribute to matters beyond (and larger than) our own self-interest.

- Purpose is directed at accomplishments, or ends, towards which one can make progress. The ends may be material or nonmaterial, and they may be reachable or non-reachable. The essential characteristic of the ends is not their concreteness or attainability but the sense of direction they provide.

Of course, purposes—even long-lasting, exhilarating ones—are not always noble. Great evil has been done by people who commit themselves to ignoble purposes. There are many ways to distinguish between noble and ignoble purposes. Perhaps the most telling way is to examine whether both the means and the ends of purpose are moral. We can easily see that the ends must be worthy: an immoral purpose such as racial or ethnic discrimination could never be noble. But the means by which we pursue our ends also must be moral if the purpose is to be a noble one. It would not be noble to pursue the eradication of world poverty by exterminating people who are poor: the end may be noble, but not the means. Nor would it be noble to attain any lofty goal by lying, by cheating, or by any other disreputable means.

To qualify as a noble purpose, the *why* of the deed as well as its *how* must be guided by a strong moral sense. Finding noble purpose means devoting ourselves to something worth doing and doing it in an honorable manner.

PURPOSE AT WORK:
DISCOVERING YOUR CALLING

The word "calling" has such a high-sounding ring to it that many people fear that it may never apply to themselves. When asked what their vocation is, they may answer "plumber," "cabdriver," "homemaker," "businessman," and so on, but then they may say something like: "But it's just a job, I don't think I can say that it's a real calling." It may surprise them to know that, linguistically at least, saying that you have a vocation means the same thing as saying that you have a calling: the term "vocation" comes from the Latin *vocatio,* "to be called."

Linguistic roots do not always translate into psychological experience. Yet we should take the original meaning of the

The most important thing people wish
to satisfy cannot be generalized
because it is as unique to every person
as an individual's DNA.
There is no more beautiful thing
in the universe than the human person.
What shows each of us
to be distinctive is the trajectory of
the calling we pursue, like the meteorites
across the night sky of history.

—MICHAEL NOVAK

word "vocation" as an indicator that it is always within our powers to turn our jobs into true callings.

The idea of a "calling" is an ancient notion with religious roots. Max Weber wrote that a calling is a "task set by God." All individuals have their own particular callings, reflecting three realities: (1) their own God-given abilities; (2) the world's need for the services that their callings provide; and (3) their enjoyment in serving society and God in their own special ways. Much like any noble purpose, a calling is both meaningful to the self and important to the world beyond the self. Christian theologian Frederick Buechner writes, "The kind of work God usually calls you to do is the kind of work (a) that you need most to do and (b) that the world most needs to have done. . . . The place God calls you to is the place where your deep gladness and the world's deep hunger meet."[3]

When you think of your work as a calling rather than merely as a "job," it transforms your entire experience of it.

It becomes possible to take pride in your most routine accomplishments, because you become aware of their contributions to the social good. Chores that once felt like drudgery become valued steps on the path towards making a difference in other people's lives. Ordinary tasks take on an exalted glow. The feelings of frustration that accompany the inevitable obstacles and setbacks of work will vanish when you realize that the primary aim of your calling is to serve and not to seek approval or other egoistic rewards.

Experiencing your work as a calling is in itself a great reward. In terms of the personal satisfaction it leads to, this reward far surpasses any material prizes that success may bring. If you don't believe that your work is a calling, in the end, all your success will feel barren and unfulfilling. By accepting your work as a calling, you can find the noble purpose in even the humblest of occupations. That sense of noble purpose will make many of your working moments shine with pleasure.

 16

This principle applies to workers in white-collar and blue-collar jobs, in the private and public sectors, and in companies large and small. It applies to people at the beginning of their careers, to people in their working primes, and to those who are winding down towards retirement. And it is contagious: workers who feel a sense of calling inspire others to find the deeper meaning in their own work.

Some years ago I was invited to visit a town that was having trouble with many of its youth. The town was affluent, so there was little need for students to take part-time jobs, but a few did anyway. One of the parents told me that her son, and some of his friends as well, had dramatically improved their behavior after going to work at a local restaurant. Intrigued, I went to see the manager. The place was a fast-food shop, serving distinctly non-gourmet fare quickly to masses of customers. Still, the manager couldn't have been more pleased with his work if he were the main chef at a five-star French bistro.

The secret of success is constancy of purpose.

—Benjamin Disraeli

The only failure a man ought to fear
is failure of cleaving to the purpose
he sees to be best.

—George Eliot

"We give folks the food they enjoy at a price they can afford, and make it possible for them to get on with their lives without aggravation and delay," he told me. "Families come here and go away in a better mood—the kids have fun, mom and dad don't have to cook or take out a mortgage on their home to pay the check."

What about his young employees? "They always start here with an attitude. They think the customers are creeps and their job is to give them the minimum they can get away with and then head out to the rear for a smoking break. I tell them that every customer *has to be* just as important to you as your closest friend. Your job isn't just to get them their food and take their money. Your job is to put a smile on each customer's face. When these kids get that, it changes everything about their attitude. They get a kick out of what they're doing, just like I do."

From what I could tell from speaking with parents in that town, the lesson that those kids learned on that job generalized

A life without purpose is
a languid, drifting thing;
Every day we ought to review
our purpose, saying to ourselves:
This day let me make
a sound beginning,
for what we have hitherto
done is naught!

—THOMAS À KEMPIS

far beyond the fast-food joint. It heightened their motivation at school, improved their behavior in their community, and elevated their feelings about who they are. The manager's joy in his work speaks for itself.

At the top of the big-business ladder, the experience of a calling is much the same. I have interviewed dozens of corporate chieftains who are convinced that their pursuit of noble purpose in their work was not only their most important source of personal satisfaction but also the key to their success. Norm Augustine, retired CEO of Lockheed Martin, told me: "I was trying to build the greatest aerospace company in the world. . . . You have to have a more lofty goal than making money. . . . To give meaning to your work, one has to enjoy what they're doing. They won't be very good at it if they don't, probably. And secondly, I think you have to feel that you're contributing something worthwhile."

One of the finer ironies of life is that the dedication to a

Your work is to discover your work and then
with all your heart to give yourself to it.

—THE BUDDHA

Providence has nothing good
or high in store for one
who does not resolutely aim
at something high or good.
A purpose is the eternal condition
of success.

—T. T. MUNGER

noble purpose usually leads to greater success, even in a worldly sense, than the narrow pursuit of baser rewards for their own sake. C. William Pollard, chairman and CEO of ServiceMaster, said in an interview: "For most, the firm is all about maximizing profits. From my perspective, it cannot and should not be the sole purpose of the firm. When it is, I believe that it is ultimately self-destructive, because I do not think you can generate profits without people; if people do not have a purpose and meaning beyond generating profits, you will come up against the law of diminishing returns. In the long run, you are not going to have consistent production of quality products and services unless people see a mission beyond profit. People work for a cause, not just a living."[4] When my research team interviewed William Pollard, he told us that what brought meaning to his work was his goal of fostering the development of those who work in his company. He told us, "So as I've seen people grow as individuals, grow in who they're becoming as well as in what they're doing, grow as parents, grow as contributors in their community or contributors in their churches or places of worship, grow as healthy citizens, all those things are fulfilling to me and bring meaning to the fact that work results in that."

Working for a cause endows you with a zeal that can be unstoppable. If the cause is a noble one, humanity benefits as you reach your goal.

In a career, the cause can remain constant even as a worker searches for his or her own best way to serve the cause. This can mean adopting new strategies, changing jobs, or even switching careers in order to find what *you* are called to do in service of the cause you believe in. A calling is one's own very particular way of finding noble purpose in an occupation. We all must find the occupation that best suits our own talents, because that will always prove to be the best way to accomplish our ultimate goals.

As part of his devotion to God's purpose, Sir John Templeton believes in the love of all humanity. In his youth, he first considered becoming a minister, but while in college, he decided that his gifts were in financial analysis and that he could best serve God and humanity in this way. He told me in an interview that his only regret is that he did not start his mutual funds earlier, "because I would have served many more people." Central to Templeton's beliefs is the idea that all people are "only the tiniest part of God"; therefore, "each of us should try to love every human being without *any* exceptions, and not just a little bit, but unlimited love for every human being with absolutely no exceptions." It follows, he continued, that separating people by tribe, race, club, nation, is "not as healthy" as thinking of all humanity as one. He expressed this vision by founding a truly international, boundary-crossing approach to global investing. The approach seemed risky and audacious at the time, but it proved brilliantly successful over

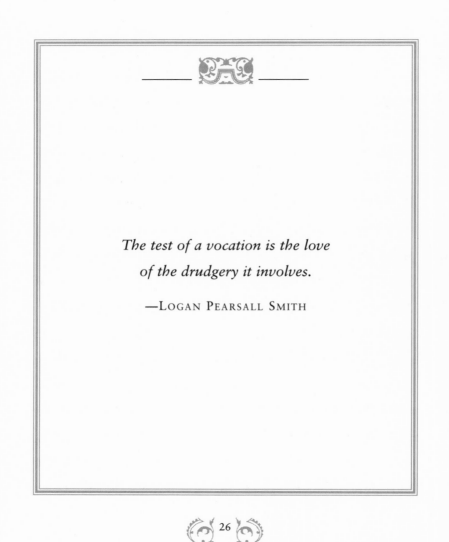

The test of a vocation is the love
of the drudgery it involves.

—Logan Pearsall Smith

time. Sir John Templeton's material success followed from his lifelong pursuit of a noble purpose—serving *all* humanity—even as he tailored his particular way of pursuing this purpose to suit his own particular gifts.

Sometimes people make such a choice voluntarily, by consciously identifying their own strengths and weaknesses, but at other times, it is forced upon them. We do not always get what we want in life, and often that works out for the best. We may be turned down for one job and end up with another that we find more profitable and more inspiring. As an ancient Irish maxim tells us, "When one door closes, another opens."

When I was a student, I dreamed of being a journalist, because I treasured the purpose of discovering the truth and informing the public about it. Soon after graduating from college, I interviewed for a writing job at a well-known newspaper and was rejected outright. (Later I found out that the editor was put off by the way I dressed—I had worn the one suit I owned,

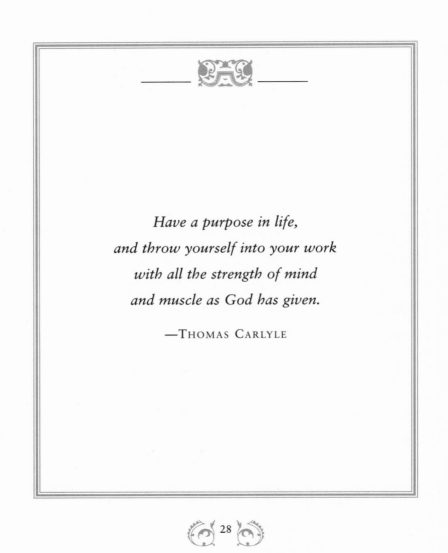

Have a purpose in life,
and throw yourself into your work
with all the strength of mind
and muscle as God has given.

—THOMAS CARLYLE

rather than "dressing down" like all his reporters, naively giving him the impression that I was not a "man of the people"!) Instead, I enrolled in a graduate program in developmental psychology, which enabled me to do exactly what I had always wanted to do—discover the truth and write about it—in a way that more closely suited my bent towards scientific analysis and my interest in human development in all its forms. Amazingly, in the last few years one of my research projects has led me into an extended engagement in journalism education, bringing me back in a very direct way to the object of my first career love. Callings work in strange and mysterious ways.

Disappointments and rejections in a career can be turned into assets if we keep in mind the big picture—that we should be pursuing a lifelong calling that goes beyond the province of any one job. Charles Harper Jr., now the executive director and senior vice president of the Templeton Foundation, has written

If you don't know
what your passion is,
realize that one reason
for your existence
on earth is to find it.

—OPRAH WINFREY

about feeling "blocked" in the pursuit of his calling—the integration and promotion of excellence in religion and science—when he spent ten difficult years as a frustrated research scientist: "For me, it led to very serious despair. I thought that it was a total waste in the end."[5] But he soon learned that this "very pursuing of what I thought was my calling is what God eventually used, though first He blocked my way and had me do other things." Harper now manages ambitious Foundation programs that seek to accomplish precisely the integration of excellent science and religion that he has always sought.

Our world is full of such stories—you can find them by simply looking around you to the inspired workers you know among your friends and family. One moving story that Harper relates is the case of Paul Brand, who became known for the prophylactic tools that he designed to make the daily movements of lepers safer and easier. Brand grew up the child of missionaries in India, and he always aspired to the noble purpose of healing lepers. But his aspirations were "blocked," at least temporarily, when he was unable to get into medical school. He took a job as a carpenter and bricklayer, learning a host of physical engineering skills. Later, when he was finally able to enter the medical profession, he turned these precise skills towards the task of creating tools that could help lepers make better use of their damaged fingers, toes, and eyesight. The enforced interlude prior to his medical training gave Paul Brand the skills he needed to achieve his noble purpose. Callings work in strange and mysterious ways.

PURPOSE CAN BE FOUND EVERYWHERE

J ust as all people can find noble purpose in their work by experiencing what they do as a calling, so, too, can people find noble purpose in any other activity or setting that the world has to offer. Family, friendship, community, the natural world within our human reach, and the cosmos beyond it—all can be arenas for our search for noble purpose. Noble purposes are all around us, in things near and far, foreign and familiar, ordinary and extraordinary. All we need to do is get in touch with the activities and settings that have the deepest meanings for us. It is up to each of us to find our own personal place in the omnipresent causes that have essential roles for us all.

As long as anyone believes that
his ideal and purpose is outside him,
that it is above the clouds,
in the past or in the future,
he will go outside himself
and seek fulfillment
where it cannot be found.
He will look for solutions
and answers at every point
except where they can
be found—in himself.

—ERICH FROMM

Some of these phrases—"deep meaning," "noble purpose," "omnipresent causes"—may sound high-blown, daunting, perhaps a bit forbidding. If so, it's the fault of the language that I have used to speak of such things. In reality, the pursuit of noble purposes can be a wonderfully plain and simple affair, played out in every moment of the most ordinary of days.

Just this morning I had my radio tuned to a local call-in show, and I heard the following tale. A woman relayed that some years ago she was eating breakfast at a coffee shop when she noticed that a young man and a woman whom she knew—but who did not know each other—had just walked in. She knew that both were shy, and she described herself as "a great believer in the power of loving relationships to cure what ails the world." The woman then determined that she would introduce these two lonely people to one another. She grabbed a table in the crowded shop and ordered some extra muffins. Then she asked the young man and woman if they would keep

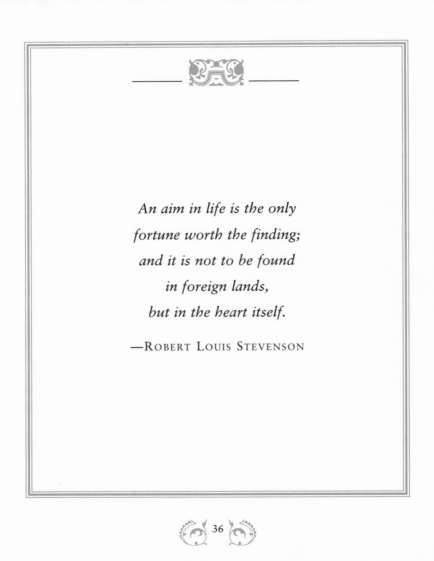

An aim in life is the only
fortune worth the finding;
and it is not to be found
in foreign lands,
but in the heart itself.

—Robert Louis Stevenson

her company and help her eat the extra food she had ordered, not mentioning that she had done so intentionally. Now, years later, the woman was calling the radio show to announce that she had just received a note from the couple—as she does regularly, on the occasion of the couple's wedding anniversaries—saying, "Thank you, we're still together." The woman's noble purpose was accomplished for the price of a few muffins.

Anthropologists who have studied many cultures sometimes joke that "three Ps" can sum up the life tasks to which people everywhere dedicate themselves: protect, provide, and procreate. This is reminiscent of T. S. Eliot's poetic witticism: "Birth, and copulation, and death / That's all the facts when you come down to brass tacks."[6] Such comments are amusing precisely because we know that while these are indeed essential life tasks, people all over the world dedicate themselves to a host of other purposes. (T. S. Eliot himself was a highly devout Christian who very much believed in purposes beyond basic

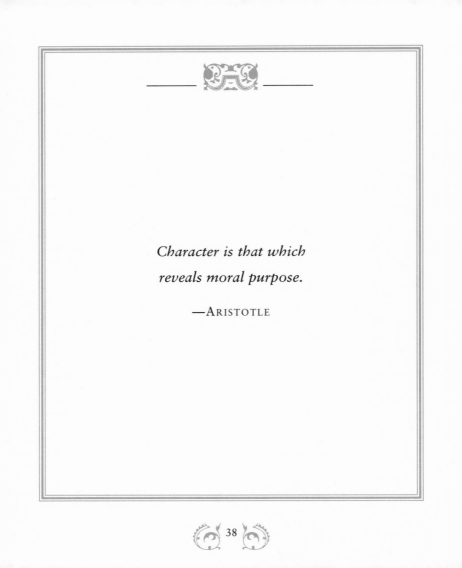

Character is that which
reveals moral purpose.

—ARISTOTLE

survival.) Some purposes are mundane; others are elevated. With the right attitude, they all can be inspiring.

Where in our lives can we find a venue to pursue purpose? There are five places where people all over the world commonly seek purpose. One is in their work, as we have discussed earlier. The four others are:

● FAMILY: At any age, a person can contribute to the well-being of the family. A child can help out around the house, chip in on necessary day-to-day-chores, keep an elderly relative company, cooperate with parental directives. Adults can start their own families, act as supportive and loyal partners to their spouses, and raise a new generation in a caring and responsible manner. Each and every one of these purposes contributes immeasurably to the present and future splendor of the world, yet we can pursue them with deeds that seem so normal that they often go unnoticed.

• COMMUNITY: Beyond our families, we have friends, neighbors, fellow citizens in the communities where we reside. What does it mean to be a good friend, a good neighbor, or a good citizen? The answer is the same in all cases: *service and engagement*. People who always say "I don't want to get involved" when trouble arises lose the precious opportunity to find meaning as members of communities. In fact, the very definition of community in sociological terms is "a group of people who feel reciprocal obligation to one another." When you feel responsible to cheer up a friend when she is down, to alert your neighbor to a leak in his roof, to cast a vote in your local elections, you are accepting your responsibilities as a friend, a neighbor, a citizen. You are finding purpose as an active member of your community.

• THE NATURAL WORLD—AND THE EXTRATERRESTRIAL UNIVERSE BEYOND: Have you ever used the phrase "communing with nature"? Some people who go out to the country and lose themselves in the grandeur of the natural world describe their experiences in this way. It is a revealing choice of words because nature, too, can be our community. We can participate as "members," because as humans we are parts of the natural world ourselves. We can learn about, appreciate, treasure, and take responsibility for the well-being of our natural "community." We can even explore the worlds beyond our immediate knowledge by gazing at the stars, imaging the infinity of the universe, and partaking in scientific studies of the cosmos. We can share with other explorers the purposes of discovery, love of nature, and preservation of its glory. From the well-designed patterns of the smallest flower to the grand designs of planetary and stellar configurations, we can glean intimations of a purpose far beyond our own limited purview.

The man without a purpose
is like a ship without a rudder—
waif, a nothing, a no man.
Have a purpose in life,
and, having it, throw
such strength of mind
and muscle into your work
as God has given you.

—THOMAS CARLYLE

• FAITH: For all of recorded history, people have devoted themselves with at least as much passion to the supernatural world as to the human and natural worlds. In its highest form, this devotion can become a committed faith that galvanizes one's entire life. In all of the world's religions, faith puts people in touch with God's purpose. With faith, the search for noble purpose becomes a direct matter of discovering God's will for us. There may be many answers to this pursuit, they may evolve and even change over a lifetime, but the search for God's will provides a stabilizing and uplifting force in one's life through all the periods of tumultuous questioning, reflection, and growth. Faith is the ultimate expression of noble purpose because its very presence brings us beyond ourselves to reach towards a transcendent aim.

There are other realms of noble purpose as well, some of which may be pursued in your spare time, during leisure

If we don't stand for something,
we may fall for anything.

—MALCOLM X

activities or voluntary service. People who take up hobbies such as art and music make the world a more beautiful place as they refine their craft. A colorful picture on someone's wall or a tune on the piano, no matter how amateurish, can brighten up the day for the rest of us. People who read to the blind, mentor a disadvantaged child, or bring food to the needy can make all the difference in the world to those whom their charity touches. Even small acts of graciousness, such as holding a door for an elderly person or giving up a seat on a crowded bus for a pregnant woman, can leave a wealth of good feelings behind. The bumper sticker that reads: COMMIT UNNECESSARY ACTS OF RANDOM KINDNESS is one prescription for achieving noble purpose in low-key, everyday ways.

There is broad cultural variation in the places where people around the world seek and discover noble purpose. Once when I was conducting research in a small Latin American fishing village, I was struck by the life plans and goals of the young

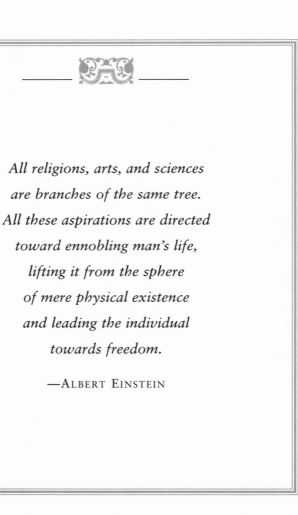

*All religions, arts, and sciences
are branches of the same tree.
All these aspirations are directed
toward ennobling man's life,
lifting it from the sphere
of mere physical existence
and leading the individual
towards freedom.*

—ALBERT EINSTEIN

people whom I observed. They were extremely family oriented, much more so than comparable groups of youngsters whom I had studied in the United States. High on their list of aspirations was to take good care of *all* members of their extended families, including grandparents, aunts, and uncles. They were committed to their communities and felt an interdependence with their friends and family that would be unusual in, say, Connecticut or California. These young people, although hardly affluent, had little desire to surpass their parents or move out of their village to greener pastures elsewhere. Their fondest desires were to become like their parents, contribute to the cultural and community life that they were born into, and support the family members who needed their help. This certainly stands as a noble purpose for these young people, although it is quite different from the more competitive ambitions that move the young in parts of the world where the desire for upward mobility reigns.

Cultural meanings can powerfully shape our aspirations as well as our sense of what is desirable. Purpose is a universal concept, but its expression often differs across cultures. Within the bounds of decency and goodness, there is a respected place in this world for cultural visions of myriad sorts.

Some cultures emphasize individuals' autonomous choices in choosing purposes for themselves, whereas other cultures emphasize the ultimate determinism of a divine plan. (Of course, even within a homogenous culture, people may depart from the normative belief system and adopt ideas from outside that culture, but, for most people, the culture that they grow up in exerts a powerful influence throughout life.) Purpose in some cultures is defined by achieving success in one's self-defined goals; in others, it is closely linked to the collective goals of the family or community.

Traditional cultures offer purposes that differ in some ways from those in contemporary cultures. In a traditional culture, purpose may be found in ancient, fixed social roles that define a person's responsibilities to key social and religious institutions. One example of this is the social institution of the family, which in traditional societies has set sex roles that designate the ways in which males and females seek purpose. For males, purpose comes from their roles as protectors and providers, whereas for females, purpose comes from their roles as mothers and caregivers. From early ages, males and females are prepared for these sex-related roles. Many traditional cultures then seal this preparation with initiation rites as soon as the child reaches puberty. In contrast, modern cultures are marked by a diverse assortment of purposes for both males and females, and the period of adolescence is seen as a time of selection and personal identity formation rather than as one of initiation and induction into predefined roles.

In some cultures, a social sense of purpose is synonymous with personal growth. Hindu-Brahmin-Indian cultures that

 49

*I have learned, that if
one advances confidently
in the direction of his dreams,
and endeavors to live
the life he has imagined,
he will meet with a success
unexpected in common hours.*

—HENRY DAVID THOREAU

believe in reincarnation, for example, recognize self-perfection as a master motive, because when individuals improve themselves, they are simultaneously advancing society's goals and God's design. In this case, advancing a social purpose means working towards personal improvement.

The anthropologist Richard Shweder has written that cultures emphasize to varying degrees the following three "ethics:" (1) the ethic of community (caring for families, nations, and other groups); (2) the ethic of autonomy (promoting individuality, rights, freedom of choice, and personal welfare); and (3) the ethic of divinity (advancing the spiritual self, fostering faith, piety, and mental or physical purity).[7] In a collective culture, like the one that exists in traditional parts of Japan, community is salient, and purposes tend to reflect this ethic. In a religious culture, like that which exists in parts of India, the ethic of divinity is salient. In the individualistic culture that prevails in many parts of the United States, the ethic of autonomy is more evident. People growing up in these cultures are by no means limited by these ethics—many Americans, for example, devote themselves to community and divinity; many Japanese and Indians choose purposes that reflect autonomy—but everyone's cultural heritage is important in providing the grounding of beliefs from which each person's later options develop. For this reason, as you search for your calling or for any other purpose in life, it is helpful to get in touch with your cultural roots so you can understand the beliefs that may have shaped your outlook and the values that may still be influencing your dreams and aspirations.

NOBLE PURPOSE REQUIRES HUMILITY

Whenever I speak in public about the importance of purpose in life, someone always asks me a very good—and hard—question, one that may have occurred to you, too, while reading what I have written in this book: Can't purpose be dangerous when employed in the wrong way? And I answer, yes, just as the right kinds of purpose can be powerful forces for the good, the wrong kinds can be horribly destructive. People who intentionally fly airplanes full of passengers into buildings may be full of purpose, but we would not call it *noble* purpose. That is why we always must take great care, and pay constant attention, to ensure that any purposes that we passionately pursue are indeed noble rather than ignoble ones.

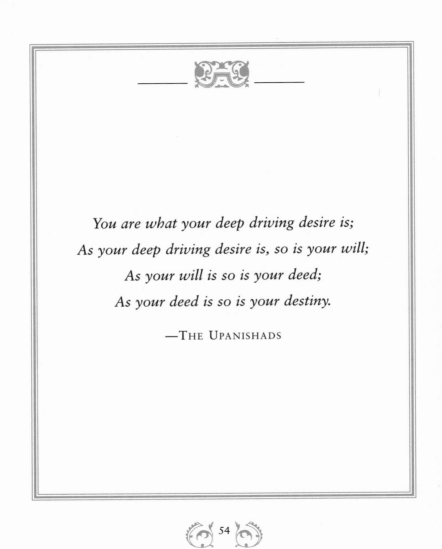

You are what your deep driving desire is;
As your deep driving desire is, so is your will;
As your will is so is your deed;
As your deed is so is your destiny.

—THE UPANISHADS

How can we do this? Certainly none of us has infallible judgment. We are human and we make mistakes. We are always at risk for trying to do something constructive and having it turn out badly for the very people and things that we wanted to support. In the face of this incertitude, how can we presume to commit ourselves to any cause?

The answer is that we must do our best, always being aware that we may be inadvertently going about things the wrong way. Such awareness is commonly called "humility." It reminds us that, no matter how noble our intentions, our capacities to do good are limited by our very humanness. A humble person is quick to self-correct when the signs indicate a wrong turn. Being willing and able to self-correct provides essential insurance against creating accidental harm. Severe damage is caused by people who heedlessly barrel ahead *after* they have been given warning that they are on a destructive course. Our most worthy leaders are bold, courageous, and

*Man's search for meaning is a primary force
in his life and not a "secondary rationalization"
of instinctual drives. This meaning is unique and
specific in that it must and can be fulfilled by him
alone; only then does it achieve a significance which
will satisfy his own will to meaning. There are some
authors who contend that meanings and values are
"nothing but defense mechanisms, reaction formations and sublimations." But as for myself, I would
not be willing to live merely for the sake of my
"defense mechanisms," nor would I be ready to die
merely for the sake of my "reaction formations."
Man, however, is able to live and even to die
for the sake of his ideals and values!*

—VIKTOR E. FRANKL

sometimes audacious in their determination to succeed, but still they are able to stay humble in their awareness of their own limitations.

Staying humble keeps our passionate commitments from boiling over into a dangerous brew of reckless zealotry. A humble commitment to a noble purpose is far preferable to either of its alternatives: no commitment to any purpose, or an arrogant belief that you have the only answer. Doing nothing is denial of hope and life itself, a waste of your potential, a loss of the opportunity that you have been given to make a positive difference for the world. And arrogance, sooner or later, leads to downfall and defeat. Purpose with humility is the best way that we humans can pursue a noble cause passionately without risking the perils of seeing our efforts do more harm than good.

In addition to the virtue of humility, there is an important moral principle that can help us keep our noble purposes from straying into ignoble territory: *The means that we employ must*

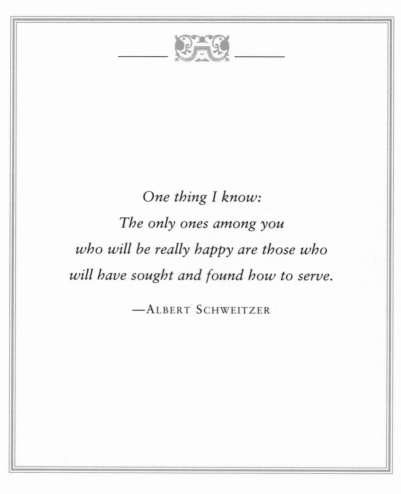

One thing I know:
The only ones among you
who will be really happy are those who
will have sought and found how to serve.

—ALBERT SCHWEITZER

be as highly moral as the ends that we pursue. Not only must our goals be directed to the benefit of the world beyond ourselves, but the way in which we accomplish them must be ethical and high-minded.

It is always tempting to compromise our principles in pursuit of a great goal, especially if we believe that the goal will improve the lot of humanity in some way. But all of history's most terrible crimes against humanity have been done in the name of some cause that was purported to improve the human condition. Anyone can profess to have a noble purpose in mind, even evil dictators and psychopathic maniacs. The best litmus test for a truly noble purpose is if it adheres to moral means. Can the purpose only be accomplished through violence and hate? Must you tell "the big lie" in order to promote your purpose? Do you need to resort to treachery to get it done? If so, your purpose is likely to be a self-serving and self-aggrandizing one rather than noble. In claiming it as a

*Firmness of purpose is one of the most
necessary sinews of character, and
one of the best instruments of success.
Without it genius wastes its efforts
in a maze of inconsistencies.*

—PHILIP DORMER CHESTERFIELD

higher cause, you are only deceiving yourself and perhaps others, too.

At a scientific meeting some years ago, I heard a public health researcher tell a story that was so poignant for him that he was choked up with emotion while relaying it. He was an ardent believer that young people should avoid developing smoking habits, and he volunteered much of his own time to visit high schools in order to relay his message to students and teachers. On one recent visit, a student asked him whether she was taking a risk by simply sitting in the presence of friends who were smoking—the phenomenon known in the public health field as "passive" or "second-hand" smoke. The researcher paused for a long time before answering. During this time, a thousand conflicting thoughts raced through his head. His first thought was that—at least at that time—he did not know of good scientific evidence that could either confirm or deny the dangers of second-hand smoke. But his next

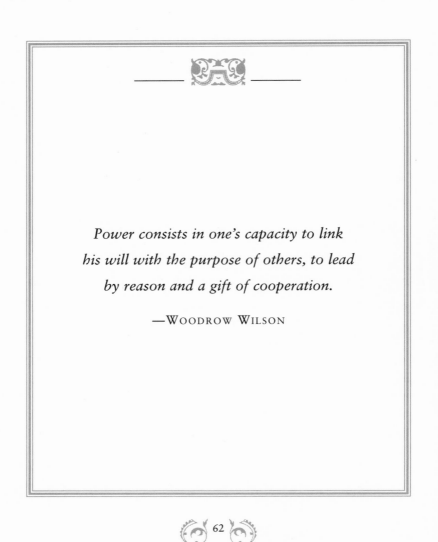

Power consists in one's capacity to link his will with the purpose of others, to lead by reason and a gift of cooperation.

—WOODROW WILSON

thought was that he didn't care about the evidence, all that was important to him was convincing these kids not to start smoking and, if possible, to tell their friends to stop if they were doing it. He was sorely tempted to go beyond his own knowledge, to exaggerate what is known about the dangers of second-hand smoke—in effect, to lie about the matter for the sake of his larger cause.

At the end of his long moment of reflection, the researcher told the student assembly the straight truth about what he knew. He could not bring himself to lie about scientific evidence, no matter how important the outcome. He said that he suffered as he made his statement, wondering if he had done the right thing. Yet later, several students came up to him and thanked him for his talk, which they obviously had found convincing and compelling. Although the researcher had given up a point of argument by sticking with the truth, he had projected the kind of credibility that gains people's trust—and high school students, of all people, are acutely sensitive to issues of adult credibility. The researcher's commitment to employ honesty, even as he agonized about its effect, advanced the noble purpose he was seeking. Ethical choices don't always yield such immediately beneficial results. But it is a sound principle of life that, in the long run, the surest way to reach a noble end is by adhering to moral means.

THE PSYCHOLOGICAL AND SPIRITUAL
SIGNIFICANCE OF PURPOSE

It has been said in many ways by many wise people that a life without purpose is a life wasted. Certainly, the converse is true: *A life built around noble purpose is a life well spent.* This is true for short lives and for long ones, for people blessed with health and for people with physical handicaps, for those with wealth and for those in less privileged circumstances, and for people to whom everything comes easily as well as for people who need to struggle in whatever they do. More than any of the physical and material conditions that they may find themselves in, devotion to purpose brings coherence and satisfaction to people's lives. Commitment to a noble purpose, apart from the good that it produces for the

65

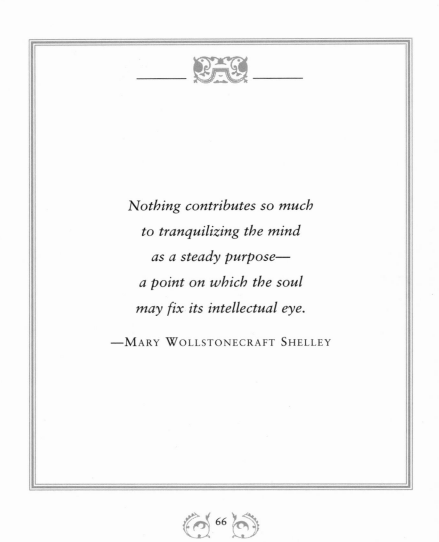

*Nothing contributes so much
to tranquilizing the mind
as a steady purpose—
a point on which the soul
may fix its intellectual eye.*

—MARY WOLLSTONECRAFT SHELLEY

world, endows a person with joy in good times and resilience in hard times.

Psychologists who study happiness repeatedly discover a puzzling paradox: the happiest people are those who pay little attention to the goal of becoming happy.[8] Many of the things that we strive for in order to become happy seem to have little to do with it. Affluence, for example, is not strongly related to happiness except in cases of severe deprivation, where more assets are needed to gain basic levels of food, shelter, and family well-being. Status, glory, and other advantages that we avidly seek do not reliably make us any happier than we were before we acquired these treasures—any boosts in mood that they create usually prove temporary, wearing off soon after the initial glow of self-congratulation. What *does* matter is engaging in something that you find absorbing, challenging, and compelling. A noble purpose is a prime example of something that creates great personal satisfaction by bringing us outside ourselves and

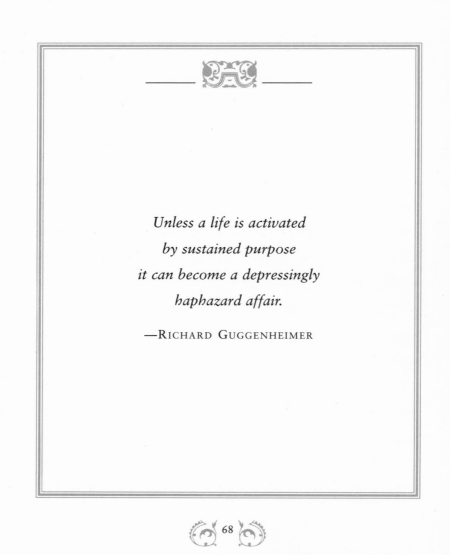

Unless a life is activated
by sustained purpose
it can become a depressingly
haphazard affair.

—RICHARD GUGGENHEIMER

into activities that capture our imaginations and promote the causes we believe in.

The paradox is that hard and often thankless effort in service of a noble purpose, with little thought of personal gain, is a surer path to happiness than the eager pursuit of happiness for its own sake. Self-indulgence simply does not work. We end up feeling empty and resentful and not at all indulged, because we have failed to satisfy our truest and deepest desires: the universal yearning for a life with meaning.

Medical and psychological research points us in the same direction. Psychologist Dan McAdams has studied adults whom he calls "generative"—people who try to make a difference in the world.[9] Generative adults are dedicated to their work, wish to leave a legacy behind, and are concerned with the well-being of future generations. McAdams's research has shown that generative adults are healthier than other adults. They are more likely to be involved in civic activities and are

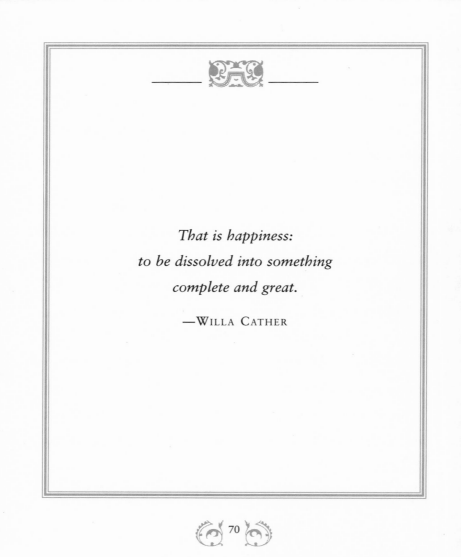

That is happiness:
to be dissolved into something
complete and great.

—WILLA CATHER

more connected to their families, churches, and political groups. They enjoy an empowered sense of self and an optimistic lens through which they view the world. They tend to believe that bad things can serve as learning opportunities and that good things will generally follow.

Purpose creates resiliency, even in the face of the most terrible events. When Hitler came to power in Germany, psychologist Victor Frankl observed the healing powers of purpose firsthand.[10] The Nazis murdered Frankl's wife, parents, and grandparents, and he suffered through three years of imprisonment as concentration camp inmate #119104. He endured slave labor, torture, starvation rations, and many other harsh indignities. Frankl found that only his will to make sense out of his horrific experiences and write about them in an edifying way enabled him to survive. The manuscript that he wrote and clung to like a life raft got him through his years of trial. Frankl also observed that other inmates with strong belief systems

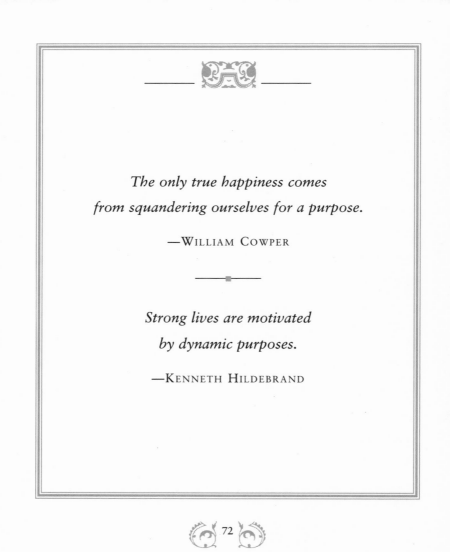

*The only true happiness comes
from squandering ourselves for a purpose.*

—WILLIAM COWPER

*Strong lives are motivated
by dynamic purposes.*

—KENNETH HILDEBRAND

endured the camp's hardships far better than those who simply tried to eke out their existence. Frankl's writings on his "search for meaning" in the midst of the Holocaust are still used by psychologists as evidence that purpose can offer people a sheltering fortress in difficult times. Frankl went on to create an approach to clinical psychology called "logotherapy" or "meaning therapy," which advanced the idea that purpose, even in normal times, promotes mental health by serving as a protective factor against depression and other anxiety disorders.

In times of war, purpose sustains civilians under attack and soldiers in combat. Wars are won or lost over the strength of a country's "morale," which is just another word for purpose. For warriors who find themselves in the direst of straights, purpose can literally be a lifesaver.

When Navy pilot James B. Stockwell was shot down over Vietnam in September 1965, he knew right away, as he later

*A useless life
is an early death.*

—GOETHE

recalled, that it was going to be "five years down there, at least."[11] Placed in solitary confinement, with a broken leg shackled in irons, Stockwell determined that he would endure by cultivating his strength and inner virtue. Bruised and ill, he started each day with one hundred sit-ups and worked throughout the day to purify his mind. He refused to do anything that would bring dishonor upon himself, his fellow prisoners, or the U.S. Navy. Stockwell's story of heroic survival has become an inspiration for millions of men and women in the armed services.

The annals of the world's great religions are full of similar stories about men and women who keep their faith despite persecution and other trials. They often say that they are full of gratitude for the hardships that have tested their faith, because all their ordeals have brought them closer to God. Their lives shine with purpose and set glowing examples for those who know them and for posterity.

Every religious tradition has discovered and advanced the great insight that the closer we come to God's purpose for us, the more satisfied we are with our lives. No matter what conception of God a person may hold, anyone can use this insight to gain a life of personal fulfillment.

CULTIVATING NOBLE PURPOSE

How can you cultivate noble purpose in your own life? Where do you find it, and how can you be sure that this is the right way to spend your time and energy?

You can start by impressing upon yourself how important it is to pursue a purpose. The case for purpose that I have made in this little book is substantiated by centuries of scientific and religious writings. Dedicating yourself to a noble purpose not only is beneficial to the world that needs your gifts, it is also essential for your own mental and spiritual health. Remind yourself of this well-documented bit of wisdom daily, and stay determined to do something about it.

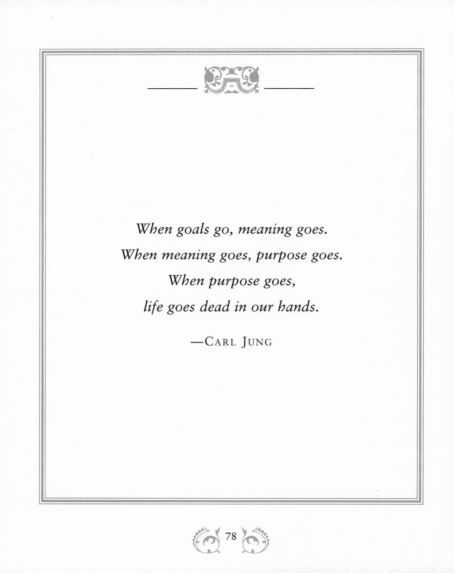

When goals go, meaning goes.

When meaning goes, purpose goes.

When purpose goes,

life goes dead in our hands.

—CARL JUNG

Here are nine principles that can facilitate a quest for purpose:

1. It is never too early to begin a life of purpose—and it is never too late. History reveals that people acquire and pursue noble purposes at many ages and in many ways. Some do it amazingly early in their lives; for example, Joan of Arc, who rallied soldiers in defense of her homeland while still a teenager. Some do it much later; for example, Anna Moses (famously known as "Grandma Moses"), who began a painting career at age seventy-five and went on to develop a unique and exquisite aesthetic style that won her international acclaim. Some come to their purposes suddenly, through dramatic conversions, like St. Paul on the road to Damascus. Others come to their purposes slowly and gradually; for example, Andrei Sakharov, who first became aware of social concerns when he witnessed an irresponsible nuclear test at age thirty-eight and then, over the following decades, adopted the broader

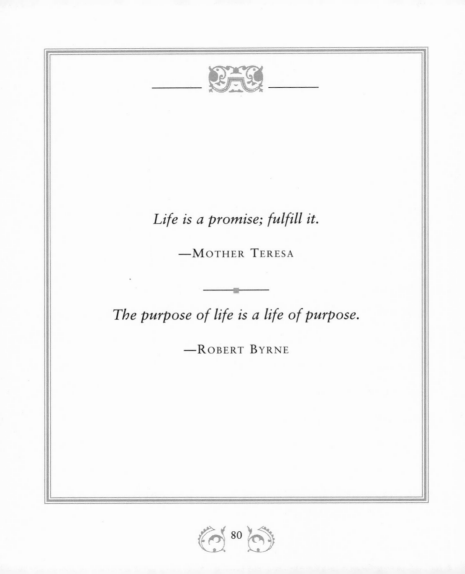

Life is a promise; fulfill it.

—MOTHER TERESA

The purpose of life is a life of purpose.

—ROBERT BYRNE

commitments to universal peace and justice that earned him a Nobel Prize. The message: Don't wait for some idealized "one right road" to purpose. There are many roads. The way that works for you is the right way.

2. Although purpose is everywhere, it may be most readily found in places that are familiar to you. Look closely at all the areas of your life—your family, your friends, your career, your avocations. Start by finding purpose in the one that you feel most engaged in at the present moment. What is your strongest suit, the part of life that you understand best, the place where you can be most sure of making a worthwhile contribution? Perhaps your quest will end there—many a meaningful life has been built around a sustained focus on a single cause. Or you may be able to use this initial experience as a base from which to extend your quest to other realms, finding purpose wherever you look and in whatever you do. Many people discover that the capacity to

discern purpose in all parts of their lives brings them closer to an awareness of God.

3. Look around for mentors—"purpose exemplars"—people who represent models of noble behavior in service of good causes. Without observing flesh-and-blood examples of the purposes that you are drawn to, you will find it difficult to decide how to go about your quest. It is impossible to guide choices by abstractions alone: no matter how high-minded or imposing the abstractions (Truth! Justice! Liberty!), in the end they will turn out sterile unless they are brought to life by real people struggling with actual problems. You can learn a great deal about how to pursue a purpose from observing these human struggles. One excellent way to do this is to develop an apprentice-like relationship with someone you admire, some-one who can mentor you in a life of purpose. Such assistance, however, may not be available to you. In that case, you can learn from the examples set by historical figures and others in

the public realm whose lives stand for the causes and principles that you believe in. Religious writings are full of inspiring biographies of saints, prophets, and men and women of faith who dedicated themselves completely to the highest of purposes.

4. When possible, get support from like-minded souls. It may be that if your purpose is obscure, ahead of its time, or unpopular, you may need to go it alone for a while. Sometimes the pursuit of a noble purpose is a lonely and unappreciated affair. But you can't be a lone wolf forever. Nor do you need to be. There are bound to be individuals or groups who share your cause. These people can provide you with much-needed feedback, counsel, and comfort in your strivings. Often they will have something to teach you; sometimes it will be the other way around. In our studies, we have found that even the greatest moral leaders at times take direction from their "followers" (in fact, it is often difficult to tell who is following whom).[12] As you pursue your purpose, you will draw strength

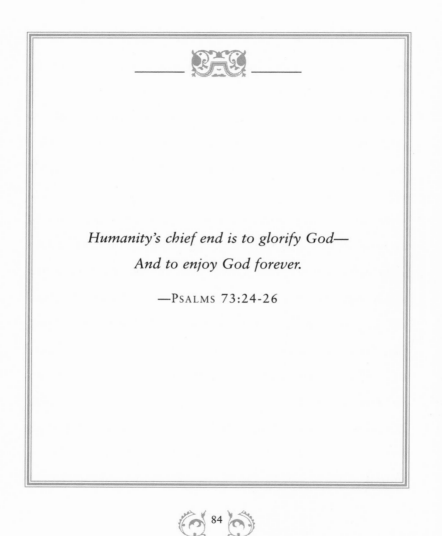

Humanity's chief end is to glorify God—
And to enjoy God forever.

—Psalms 73:24-26

from any who take the journey with you; in turn, you will add to their strengths as well.

5. Be prepared for occasional disillusionment, and resist it mightily. Anyone who harbors a lofty goal inevitably will fall short of completely attaining it. We can make progress, we can enjoy many successes, we can solve many problems, but we will never be able to fix everything that we work to fix for all time. People who dedicate themselves to ambitious causes such as alleviating poverty soon discover that no matter how much they accomplish, by the end of their labors there will still be problems such as poverty in the world. For these people, the failure to accomplish their entire purpose could lead to disillusionment if they allow themselves to flirt with perfectionism. Anyone who expects perfection in this life is bound to become disappointed—and this includes expecting perfection from ourselves. We are entitled to try our best—indeed, we are obligated to do so—but we must keep in mind

The tragedy of life doesn't lie
in not reaching your goal.
The tragedy lies in having no goal to reach.
It isn't a calamity to die with dreams unfulfilled,
but it is a calamity not to dream. . . .
It is not a disgrace not to reach the stars,
but it is a disgrace to have no stars to reach for.
Not failure, but low aim is sin.

—BENJAMIN ELIJAH MAYS

that we are only human. If we adjust our expectations accordingly, we can avert the disillusionment that comes from an inflated sense of our importance in the world. This point leads to the next principle.

6. Stay humble. When passion for a noble purpose turns into self-righteousness, we lose our capacity to learn from our mistakes or even to notice when we are making mistakes. We must always be on guard to make sure that the justifiable satisfaction that we earn with a life of purpose does not become pridefulness, which has been long been recognized, for good reason, as a deadly sin (some would say *the* most deadly sin). Pride harms us, harms those we are trying to help, and ultimately harms the purpose that we are trying to accomplish. The only way to avoid this constant danger is to keep a healthy perspective on ourselves. Although everything we do in this world matters, and our lives are of great consequence to ourselves and to others, as individuals we are of limited

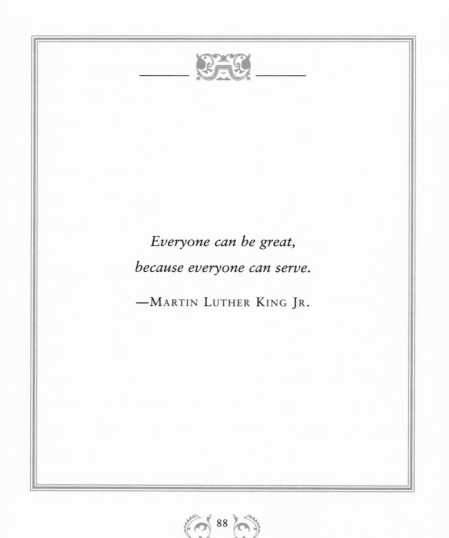

Everyone can be great,

because everyone can serve.

—Martin Luther King Jr.

importance in the larger scheme of things. This applies even to the most exalted people on the planet. In the glory days of the Roman Empire, the emperor was assigned an "advisor" to sit alongside him in his chariot when he rode along to the lusty cheers of his revering throngs. The advisor would whisper *"sic transit gloria"* in the emperor's ear—"All glory is fleeting." Often I have wished that someone would supply this special service to each of us daily.

7. Be sure that your purpose remains noble by paying attention not only to the ends that you seek but also to the means by which you pursue it. There are three questions that you can ask in order to ensure that your purpose is a noble one: (1) What am I trying to achieve; (2) Why am I trying to achieve it; and (3) How am I going about it? Many purposes that begin nobly degenerate into counterproductive forces because of a single-minded focus on the *what*. It is far easier to define a noble-sounding goal than to sustain a commitment to

I have one life and one chance
to make it count for something. . . .
I'm free to choose what that something is,
and the something I've chosen is my faith.
Now, my faith goes beyond theology and religion
and requires considerable work and effort.
My faith demands—this is not optional—
my faith demands that I do whatever I can,
wherever I am, whenever I can,
for as long as I can with whatever I have
to try to make a difference.

—Jimmy Carter

pursue it in the right way and for the right reasons. Yet if we ultimately want to do good in the world—and that, after all, is what gives our lives and our aspirations meaning—we must sustain the commitment to go about things in a moral manner, even if this makes our goal harder to reach—and it most likely will, at least in the short term. But we are in it for the long term, longer than we may live to see.

8. Celebrate your purpose, and be grateful for it. It is a gift—indeed, it is a double gift, one that you bestow to others and one that has been bestowed on you. You are fortunate to have a noble purpose, and the rest of world is fortunate that you have one. Appreciate your double good fortune! Such appreciation is pleasurable in itself, and it also brings an extra benefit: research has shown that people who feel grateful about their lives are more successful in achieving their goals and are more inclined to help others than people who lack gratitude. Moreover, appreciation fosters emotions such as awe, wonder,

elevation, and admiration, all of which get us in touch with the sublime dimensions of the cosmos.

9. Pass on your purpose to others, especially to the young. Set up apprenticeships. Get young people engaged in the noble causes that inspire you. Mentor them in the same way that you have been mentored by the exemplars whom you have admired (see no. 3 above). Young people need positive role models who can show them how to find their "callings" in their work, how to contribute to their families, how to serve their communities and their God. Young people who have mentors from their communities are in turn likely to engage in service activities on behalf of their community. Similarly, exemplars of spiritual faith can help young people discover purpose through devotional practices and disciplines. When you pass your noble purpose to a younger generation, you place the purpose in the hands of people who can pursue it with new talents, fresh energies, and their own innovative

visions. This is bound to bring the purpose closer to realization than anything you could have done on your own. It is your gift to the young, a way of helping the next generation find the meaning that you have sought, cultivated, and treasured in your own life.

NOTES

1. Csikszentmihalyi, M. (1997). *Finding flow: The psychology of engagement with everyday life.* New York: BasicBooks.

2. Damon, W., Menon, J., and Bronk, K. (2003). The development of purpose in adolescence. *Journal of Applied Developmental Science.*

3. Buechner, F. (1993). *Wishful thinking: A theological ABC.* San Francisco: Harper San Francisco, 118–119.

4. Pollard, C. W. (2000, May/June). Quoted in *Religion and Liberty, 10*(3), 1–4.

5. Harper, C. (2001). How does God lead us to our calling? *Perspectives on Science and Christian Faith, 53*(4), 225–235.

6. Eliot, T. S. (1932). *Sweeney agonistes.* London: Faber & Faber, 132.

7. Shweder, R. (2003). *Why do men barbecue?: Recipes for cultural psychology.* Cambridge, Mass.: Harvard University Press.

8. Seligman, M. (2002). *Authentic happiness.* New York: Free Press; Meyers, D. (1992). *The pursuit of happiness.* New York: Basic Books; Colby, A., and Damon, W. (1992). *Some do care: Contemporary lives of moral commitment.* New York: Free Press.

9. McAdams, D. P. (1996). *The stories we live by: Personal myths and the making of the self.* New York: Guilford Press.

10. Frankl, V. E. (1959). *Man's search for meaning: An introduction to logotherapy.* Boston: Beacon Press.

11. Stockwell, J. B. (1994). *Courage under fire.* Stanford: Hoover Institution Press.

12. Colby, A., and Damon, W. (1992). *Some do care: Contemporary lives of moral commitment.* New York: Free Press.

RECOMMENDED READINGS

Colby, Anne and William Damon. *Some do care: Contemporary lives of moral commitment.* New York: The Free Press, 1992.

Csikszentmilhalyi, Mihaly. *Finding flow: The psychology of engagement with everday life.* New York: Basic Books, 1997.

Leider, Richard J. *The power of purpose: Creating meaning in your life and work.* San Francisco: Berrett-Koehler Publishers, 1997.

Myers, David G. *The pursuit of happiness: What makes a person happy.* New York: W. Morrow, 1992.

Novak, Michael. *Business as a calling: Work and the examined life.* New York: The Free Press, 1996.

Seligman, Martin. *Authentic happiness: Using the new positive psychology to realize your potential for lasting fulfillment.* New York: The Free Press, 2002.

Templeton, Sir John M. and Rebekah Alezander Dunlap. *Why are we created? Increasing our understanding of humanity's purpose on earth.* Philadelphia: Templeton Foundation Press, 2003.